"What Michael LaPierre has do biblical source material and, in a meaningful way, connect it with the reality of today's culture. He presents a road map for Christians and churches to follow that is aligned with Scripture. He also addresses the role that 'Released Time' (biblical outreach to public school students) can play in bringing hope to our country's students. For anyone interested in looking at what the Bible says about today's culture, it is well worth reading."

— **KEN BREIVIK**, National Executive Director of School Ministries

"Throughout the pages of *A Covenant*, LaPierre challenges believers to engage the culture as salt and light. He issues a clarion call to use the truths of the Bible to inform and permeate our thinking as we examine legislation and our involvement in the public square. We must not cower or whisper in the face of withering opposition—but rather boldly proclaim truths firmly rooted in Scripture. As our Creator and the Divine Author of the Scriptures, God presents a winning formula to impact and influence the world. We never lose when our focus firmly rests in Him and eternal truth."

— **RANDY PAGE**, Chief of Staff, Office of the President at Bob Jones University

"One of the most important principles we learn in the 'Market Place Ministry' world is the principal of the priesthood of believers. In order to adequately approach public discourse and Christian civic responsibility, we must approach business and community through the eyes of a priest. What would Jesus do? And what should we do in light of God's love and grace in our lives? My prayer is that great writers and leaders like Michael LaPierre will continue to teach us how to be committed in the market place. We need to teach and develop faith leaders to be priests, trained to make an impact in our communities. Thank you, Michael, for your willingness to write, teach, and lead."

—**WILLIAM RENFROW**, SC Christian Chamber of Commerce, Chairman of the Board

"In his book *A Covenant*, Michael LaPierre has issued a clarion call for the Christian voice to re-enter its proper place in the public and civic sectors. He challenges us to 'desire and create a public, conversational domain for the glory of God.' Michael does an excellent job of building a proper worldview of how the sphere of government should properly relate to God, the family, and the church. He answers the question of how we, as Christians, should view our role in the governmental/political domain. God's Kingdom should not be limited to the fringes. On the contrary, the Kingdom of God should inform us in all domains of our existence. I highly recommend that you read this book, even multiple times, to revive your voice and resolve to spread Christian virtue in the sphere of the public domain. I will leave you with a quote from Michael: 'What our nation becomes in large part is derived by those who are willing to get involved and lead.'"

—**CHRISTOPHER L. REVELLS**, Owner/Founder of The Raphah Company

A COVENANT

*RESPONSIBLE CITIZENSHIP AND
GODLY CONVERSATION*

MICHAEL J. LAPIERRE

HIGH BRIDGE BOOKS
HOUSTON

A Covenant: Responsible Citizenship and Godly Conversation
by Michael J. LaPierre

Printed in the United States of America
ISBN (Paperback): 978-1-946615-36-7

High Bridge Books titles may be purchased in bulk for educational, business, fundraising, or sales promotional use. For information, please contact High Bridge Books via www.HighBridgeBooks.com/contact.

Published in Houston, Texas by High Bridge Books.

Unless otherwise indicated, all Scripture quotations are taken from the King James Study Bible (previously published as The Liberty Annotated Study Bible and as The Annotated Study Bible, King James Version). Copyright 1988 by Liberty University.

CONTENTS

ABOUT THE AUTHOR

Michael James LaPierre is a Brown University graduate with Bachelor of Arts degrees in both Organizational Behavior and Management and Political Science. He holds a Master of Business Administration degree from Clemson University with a focus on Entrepreneurship and Innovation. He is an author, motivational speaker, guest lecturer, and founder and current President of *Christian Leadership Worldview International, LLC* (clwi.org).

A former professional baseball player, his executive experiences over the past 30 years include VP of Sales, Director of Sales & Marketing, global strategist, entrepreneur, church servant/deacon, and community leader. His diverse executive background and nonprofit experiences have allowed him to gain a comprehensive understanding of the principles of leadership development. Those broad experiences include leadership positions on management teams in companies such as UPS, Arnold Industries, Lily Transportation, and Roadway Express.

With nonprofit, for-profit, ministerial, and athletic experiences as a backdrop, Michael has the proven ability to capture the essence and fundamentals of leadership training and development. He then relates those varied experiences in a communication style that is motivational, powerful, and relevant to today's employees, students, and organizational leaders.

Mike and his wife, Calie, have been married for more than 34 years. They have three adult children: Ryan, Kyle, and Lauren. They have also been blessed with four grandchildren: Emma, Julia, Cooper, and Tanner. Mike and Calie reside in Pickens, South Carolina.

To contact Mike about speaking at your next leadership event and/or conducting a leadership conference/seminar, you can reach him via the following:

    mikelapi@gmail.com
    mike@clwi.org
    www.clwi.org

My mouth shall shew forth thy righteousness and thy salvation all the day; for I know not the numbers thereof. I will go in the strength of the Lord GOD: I will make mention of thy righteousness, even of thine only. O God, thou hast taught me from my youth: and hitherto have I declared thy wondrous works. Now also when I am old and grayheaded, O God, forsake me not; until I have shewed thy strength unto this generation, and thy power to every one that is to come.

—PSALMS 71:15–18

The wicked flee when no man pursueth: but the righteous are bold as a lion.

—PROVERBS 28:1

And all the inhabitants of the earth are reputed as nothing: and he doeth according to his will in the army of heaven, and among the inhabitants of the earth: and none can stay his hand, or say unto him, What doest thou?

—DANIEL 4:35

ORGANIZATIONAL AFFILIATIONS

- Christian Leadership Worldview Int'l, Founder/President
- SC Christian Chamber of Commerce, Board of Directors
- Advance USA, Ambassador
- Southern Wesleyan University, Business School Board of Advisors
- Anderson University, Board of Visitors
- Clemson Chamber of Commerce, Member
- Pickens County Cattlemen's Association, Member
- Toastmasters International, Member
- Faith Baptist Church (Mentor, College and Career)
- Christian Business Men Connection (CBMC), Member
- Heritage Foundation, Member
- NRA, Member

This book is dedicated to the concerned Christian citizens and leaders of the United States of America.

FOREWORD

I HAVE BEEN ACTIVELY INVOLVED in our nation as "salt and light" (Matthew 5:13-16) for over thirty years. Former Attorney General John Ashcroft got me involved in government in the 1980s when I was pastoring a church and overseeing a Christian school in Kansas City, Missouri. Later, I worked closely with him as God allowed me to be the President of the American Association of Christian Schools for ten years. During that time, we established an office on Capitol Hill to more actively confront the Congress and the White House with the Biblical issues of the day. General Ashcroft also helped me start AdvanceUSA, an advocacy group to advance "righteousness" in the land (Proverbs 14:34), which I lead today. I have seen and continue to see the need for more born again Christians (John 3:3-7) to be involved in our government locally, in each state, and in the federal government in Washington, D.C. I have sought to be faithful in this area (1 Corinthians 4:2) and have encouraged others to join me in the cause (1 Samuel 17:29).

Recently, God caused my path to cross with Michael LaPierre, the founder of Christian Leadership Worldview International. I have seen firsthand his burden to teach biblical leadership and to get more people involved in our nation's free democratic society. The Bible tells us in Luke 19:13 to "occupy till he comes." We need to stay active in our churches, communities, and country until Jesus comes again to take his children home to heaven.

> Behold, I come quickly; and my reward is with me, to give every man according as his work shall be. (Rev. 22:12)

In this book, Michael challenges all of us to be active in the "work" of preserving and impacting our nation for Jesus Christ. I pray that God the Holy Spirit uses this book and the perfect Book, the Bible, to motivate many more people to get involved in the work of being "salt and light" the way General Ashcroft challenged me so many years ago. May this book help expand God's work and proclaim His Son until He comes again (John 14:1-3).

Please, always remember the admonition of the Apostle Paul in 1 Corinthians 10:31: "Whether therefore ye eat, or drink, or whatsoever you do, do all to the glory of God."

—Dr. Carl D. Herbster
Founder and President, AdvanceUSA

PREFACE

Lord, help me to manifest the ingredients of a salt-and light-filled life as an American citizen so that I can point others to Christ Jesus.

IS THERE ANY BETTER IMAGERY in the entire world that can more accurately depict our duty to be responsible citizens and to impact our culture than these verses in Matthew?

> Ye are the salt of the earth: but if the salt have lost his savour, wherewith shall it be salted? it is thenceforth good for nothing, but to be cast out, and to be trodden under foot of men. Ye are the light of the world. A city that is set on a hill cannot be hid. Neither do men light a candle, and put it under a bushel, but on a candlestick; and it giveth light unto all that are in the house. Let your light so shine before men, that they may see your good works, and glorify your Father which is in heaven. (Matt. 5:13-16)

These few verses capture the essence of our civic responsibility in a way that gives us a panoramic understanding of our leadership role in the public service and spiritual realms.

First, the Word of God speaks to the preserving nature of our role here on earth. As preserving agents, "salty" Christians must be willing to engage in the level of spiritual warfare required to slow down and combat the moral erosion taking place in our communities. On a larger and more national scale, God's Word is indicating to us that we should be willing to be the change agents necessary to preserve the moral fabric and godly imperatives given our great nation. We know what happens when mankind is left to his own devices. Moral apostasy prevails. Those same principles apply to the political arena. Wickedness will ensue if we leave our government to its own devices. God's moral law must be defended at every turn so that we can experience the totality of our religious freedom. When we do, life, liberty, and the pursuit of happiness will come sharply into focus. They will come into focus because we have decided to reorient our priorities back to Christ and away from the world.

We must never let the sands of humanity try to tread underfoot the excellency of the Spirit of God and His divine nature. God is telling us to let the manifestation of our Christian lights shine with a luminescence that can only be attributed to our Lord and Savior Jesus Christ. It further tells us that we should never shrink from those spiritual responsibilities. Christians must never hide, procrastinate, or put on the back burner those things that would support our citizen involvement as born-again believers. There is an expectation that we will lead out front in all of the spiritual sandboxes of life (and this includes our politics) that will be seen by the world, and they will take notice of our good works. When this happens, we immediately point skyward and give God the honor and the glory! The day has come where pride, self-sufficiency, and self-preservation must be put aside in favor of public service and a Christian leadership worldview.

God is asking Christians to be the salt and light that will help us preserve the best that man can be through the empowerment of the Holy Spirit.

> But the path of the just is as the shining light, that shineth more and more unto the perfect day. (Prov. 4:18)

The Great Physician has prescribed the holy and reverent methods of spiritual cleansing and constancy (salt and light) needed to sustain a vibrant nation. If we abandon the necessary cure for societal deterioration, we do ourselves and our countrymen great harm. We can't have it both ways. We can't enjoy the comforts attributed to us in this life without great personal sacrifice. Religious freedom, security, economic mobility, and national spiritual well-being must all be supported and undergirded with an active and enthusiastic citizenry. The activity and enthusiasm must show itself in a much bigger way than ordinary chatter and idle conversation.

Citizens of the United States of America must covenant together to be active participants in the body politic to effect real change. In other words, sitting on the sidelines of the sandbox of citizenship involvement will ruin our country and bring her to her knees. More positively stated, if we are committed to being the salt and light that Christ desires in the public arena and beyond, we will crowd out all of the contaminants in this present culture and replace them with the godly attributes of Jesus Christ our Lord! Godly conversation should also saturate every word that proceeds from our tongues.

> Let your speech be alway with grace, seasoned with salt, that ye may know how ye ought to answer every man. (Col. 4:6)

When this happens, there will be no stopping the spiritual progression and lasting moral impact on our country. Our countrymen and posterity will not soon forget our dogged determination and resolve.

INTRODUCTION

ON DECEMBER 22, 1820, Daniel Webster spoke at the bicentennial celebration of the Pilgrims landing at Plymouth Rock:

> Lastly, our ancestors established their system of government on morality and religious sentiment. Moral habits, they believed, cannot safely be trusted on any other foundation than religious principle, nor any government be secure which is not supported by moral habits ... Whatever makes men good Christians, makes them good citizens.[1]

If I could be so bold as to add to Christian Statesman Daniel Webster's comments, "It also makes them good public servants and leaders."

In this discourse, we are going to look at what the Bible has to say about our civic responsibility and how we relate to others as Christian men and women in the public arena. What conclusions can we draw from the Word of God that will give us the appropriate direction and guidance that we need as imperfect human beings serving a holy and righteous God?

As we draw those conclusions, I am going to make some broad observations and interpretations about leadership and our culture in America. These are not designed to cast dispersion or shed a negative light on any one individual. These conclusions are aimed at encouraging and challenging all Christian leaders in the church body across America. By the leading of the Holy Spirit, I am trying to help us think beyond a theoretical understanding of our responsibilities in the political arena and stir us up toward our activism in the same.

> Yea, I think it meet, as long as I am in this tabernacle, to stir you up by putting you in remembrance. (2 Pet. 1:13)

> This second epistle, beloved, I now write unto you; in both which I stir up your pure minds by way of remembrance. (2 Pet. 3:1)

> I will therefore put you in remembrance, though ye once knew this, how that the Lord, having saved the people out of the land of Egypt, afterward destroyed them that believed not. (Jude 1:5)

The Bible extends enormous responsibility in the sandbox of public policy, governance, and the corresponding decision-making in each. At certain times, as much as we would like to run and hide from the decisions in the public arena, God tells Christians to lead. The Bible tells us much more than to simply identify with Christianity in politics. We must live Christianity out loud and with the passion and vigor necessary to proclaim Christ and impact the culture.

He also reminds us that He is in control. Jesus Christ reigns supreme, and we should always take shelter in the shadow of His wings.

---

[1] Compilation by Verna M. Hall, The Christian History of the Constitution of the Unites States of America, The Foundation for American Christian Education (San Francisco, California, 1966), 177.

1

HIS SUPREMACY

Dear Lord, help me to be a faithful husbandman and citizen in the temporal assignment of ambassador that you have given me for your glory.

THE SUPREMACY OF THE "Great I Am," His mercy, and the refuge that He provides are on full display in the following verses:

> For the earth is the Lord's, and the fulness thereof. (1 Cor. 10:26)

When you read this verse is there any doubt about who is in control?

> Thou art worthy, O Lord, to receive glory and honour and power: for thou hast created all things, and for thy pleasure they are and were created. (Rev. 4:11)

We serve at the Lord's pleasure.

Be merciful unto me, O God, be merciful unto me:
for my soul trusteth in thee: yea, in the shadow
of thy wings will I make my refuge, until these
calamities be overpast. (Ps. 57:1)

Well, to say that some of the decisions being made in the
public arena are calamities would be a gross understate-
ment. But we know beyond a shadow of a doubt that God is
sovereign and reigns supreme over every spiritual and
physical realm, which includes ministry, family, vocation,
education, arts and entertainment, athletics, and, yes, even
our governance.

Illustration 1.1

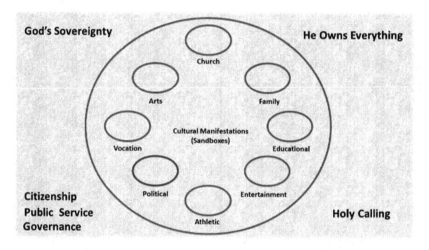

This illustration shows us that God owns all of the spir-
itual sandboxes in which we live. He uses each of these for
His will, to prepare Christians spiritually, to give glory to
His name, and to help believers learn how to love their

neighbors. Are Christians today impacting each of these primary spiritual sandboxes? Is God the primary focus in each? If not, why not?

There are two more questions that must be asked. Why have we ceded control of our politics to secular humanism? How and why has the enemy made so many inroads into controlling this spiritual realm?

First, we are going to look at specific scriptural references that help us understand our civic responsibility. Second, we will explore the cultural conditions that exist in America to help explain our current plight. Finally, let us create a traditional and historical road map from the Bible and our Christian forefathers to pave an exciting new path ahead (well, really an old path that we are going to recommission for His glory). The verses in the following section will give us both direct and indirect application and the necessary context, while providing the springboard of understanding relating to our civic responsibilities in the 21st century.

2

Civic Responsibility and the Bible

God, show us from your Word how you would
organize our thinking on this issue.

GOD'S WORD AND HIS moral law are the foundation of this Covenant. They should sanitize the sin and iniquity ingrained in our current political system. His Word and moral law should also help us see through and discern the baser instincts of power, pride, and self-preservation for those seeking positions of leadership and higher authority. In other words, we should be very leery of anything or anyone that resembles lofty human thinking and pride. Every aspect of public life for Christians should be pointed skyward to glorify His name. Let's consider the following foundational verses that are key to the totality of our understanding on this issue.

> Let every soul be subject unto the higher powers.
> For there is no power but of God: the powers that

be are ordained of God. Whosoever therefore resisteth the power, resisteth the ordinance of God:
and they that resist shall receive to themselves
damnation. For rulers are not a terror to good
works, but to the evil. Wilt thou then not be
afraid of the power? do that which is good, and
thou shalt have praise of the same: For he is the
minister of God to thee for good. But if thou do
that which is evil, be afraid; for he beareth not the
sword in vain: for he is the minister of God, a re-
venger to execute wrath upon him that doeth
evil. Wherefore ye must needs be subject, not
only for wrath, but also for conscience sake. For
this cause pay ye tribute also: for they are God's
ministers, attending continually upon this very
thing. Render therefore to all their dues: tribute
to whom tribute is due; custom to whom custom;
fear to whom fear; honour to whom honour.
(Rom. 13:1–7)

The Word of God tells Christians to submit themselves
to those in governmental authority and honor them because
they have been appointed and ordained by God for our
good.

All the ends of the world shall remember and
turn unto the LORD: and all the kindreds of the
nations shall worship before thee. For the kingdom is the LORD's: and he is the governor among
the nations. (Ps. 22:27–28)

God is ultimately our supreme ruler, sovereign, and governor over our political system.

> By me kings reign, and princes decree justice. (Prov. 8:15)

He directs and controls every minute detail of governance and justice here on Earth.

> The king's heart is in the hand of the LORD, as the rivers of water: he turneth it whithersoever he will. (Prov. 21:1)

This verse is further proof of the omniscient, omnipresent, and omnipotent character of God, who *actively* controls earthly matters of governance.

> When thou sittest to eat with a ruler, consider diligently what is before thee: And put a knife to thy throat, if thou be a man given to appetite. (Prov. 23:1–2)

Mankind ought to have a higher element of decency and decor in the presence of a king … it is called respect.

> Then Peter and the other apostles answered and said, *We ought to obey God rather than men.* (Acts 5:29, emphasis mine)

The hierarchy of allegiance and the corresponding obedience is clearly defined in the Bible.

Redeeming the time, because the days are evil. (Eph. 5:16)

Christians have a responsibility to impact the culture in which they live with activist pursuits for the glory of God.

If thou seest the oppression of the poor, and violent perverting of judgment and justice in a province, marvel not at the matter: for he that is higher than the highest regardeth; and there be higher than they. (Eccl. 5:8)

God sees all travesty of injustice in the world, including our political arena.

I counsel thee to keep the king's commandment, and that in regard of the oath of God. Be not hasty to go out of his sight: stand not in an evil thing; for he doeth whatsoever pleaseth him. Where the word of a king is, there is power: and who may say unto him, What doest thou? Whoso keepeth the commandment shall feel no evil thing: and a wise man's heart discerneth both time and judgment. (Eccl. 8:2–5)

The Bible instructs us to submit to the higher powers of authority in our land.

Shall the throne of iniquity have fellowship with thee, which frameth mischief by a law? They gather themselves together against the soul of the righteous, and condemn the innocent blood. But the LORD is my defence; and my God is the rock of my refuge. And he shall bring upon them their own iniquity, and shall cut them off in their own wickedness; yea, the LORD our God shall cut them off. (Ps. 94:20–23)

Wicked forms of government will not stand — a serious and disturbing thought when we search for the United States in the discussion of the end times in the book of Revelation.

Submit yourselves to every ordinance of man for the Lord's sake: whether it be to the king, as supreme; Or unto governors, as unto them that are sent by him for the punishment of evildoers, and for the praise of them that do well. For so is the will of God, that with well doing ye may put to silence the ignorance of foolish men: As free, and not using your liberty for a cloke of maliciousness, but as the servants of God. Honour all men. Love the brotherhood. Fear God. Honour the king. (1 Pet. 2:13–17)

We must submit ourselves to the laws of the land and those that govern over us as servants of God, regardless of their level of influence.

Put them in mind to be subject to principalities and powers, to obey magistrates, to be ready to every good work, To speak evil of no man, to be no brawlers, but gentle, shewing all meekness unto all men. (Titus 3:1–2)

When submitting to the powers of government, we are to do so with the grace and peace that exudes Christ Jesus.

> And they watched him, and sent forth spies, which should feign themselves just men, that they might take hold of his words, that so they might deliver him unto the power and authority of the governor. And they asked him, saying, Master, we know that thou sayest and teachest rightly, neither acceptest thou the person of any, but teachest the way of God truly: Is it lawful for us to give tribute unto Caesar, or no? But he perceived their craftiness, and said unto them, Why tempt ye me? Shew me a penny. Whose image and superscription hath it? They answered and said, Caesar's. And he said unto them, Render therefore unto Caesar the things which be Caesar's, and unto God the things which be God's. And they could not take hold of his words before the people: and they marvelled at his answer, and held their peace. (Luke 20:20–26)

Christ himself skillfully discerns the powers of governance from the powers on high along with their respective levels of authority.

> And when they were come to Capernaum, they that received tribute money came to Peter, and said, Doth not your master pay tribute? He saith, Yes. And when he was come into the house, Jesus

prevented him, saying, What thinkest thou, Simon? of whom do the kings of the earth take custom or tribute? of their own children, or of strangers? Peter saith unto him, Of strangers. Jesus saith unto him, Then are the children free. Notwithstanding, lest we should offend them, go thou to the sea, and cast an hook, and take up the fish that first cometh up; and when thou hast opened his mouth, thou shalt find a piece of money: that take, and give unto them for me and thee. (Matt. 17:24–27)

Christ modeled our responsibility to pay taxes and give to the government their requested portion.

There are dozens and dozens of additional verses of Scripture that set the stage for both our understanding and the necessary execution of our civic responsibilities. For those who would like to do further research, the following verses provide additional support: Mark 12:13–17, Matthew 22:15–22, 1 Timothy 2:1–2, Daniel 2:20–21, Deuteronomy 16:18–20, Revelation 1:5–6, John 19:11, Mark 3:24, and Colossians 2:15.

3

OUR CULTURE

Lord Jesus, help me to understand my specific role in impacting our culture.

HOW DOES OUR BIBLE RESPONSIBILITY in the political arena coincide with the current culture? What about our leadership responsibilities in general? How do they relate to the political realm?

Illustration 1.2

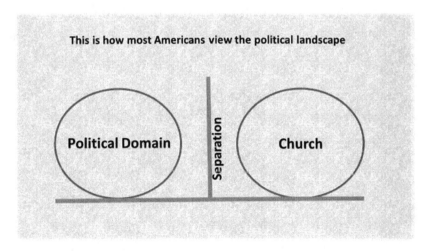

This is how most Americans view the political landscape

Political Domain   Separation   Church

Separation of church and state is destroying our country. The Secular Humanist version of separation of church and state is effectively draining our country of its spiritual vibrancy. Dysfunction abounds. We are being lulled to sleep with the choruses and lullabies of humanity. Unfortunately, most Americans currently look at both politics and the church on the same horizontal plane, giving them equal weight and little distinction.

In the world's eyes and among many Christians, these spiritual "sandboxes" are simply providing different functionality and utility. In other words, Christians have the ability to consume what they need in each sandbox with very little reverence given to His church. America has been brainwashed (indoctrinated) into thinking that this is normal and that we can do nothing about it. Beyond that, our young people think that this version of America *is* America, not understanding the undermining influences that have been at work to get us to this point. This is not the America that I see in the early development of our country.

It is a well-known fact that in America, the Christian consensus that once existed on our shores has vanquished. The slow and steady descent of our morality as a nation is quite evident.

> This know also, that in the last days perilous times shall come. For men shall be lovers of their own selves, covetous, boasters, proud, blasphemers, disobedient to parents, unthankful, unholy, Without natural affection, trucebreakers, false accusers, incontinent, fierce, despisers of those that are good, Traitors, heady, highminded, lovers of pleasures more than lovers of God;

Having a form of godliness, but denying the
power thereof: from such turn away. For of this
sort are they which creep into houses, and lead
captive silly women laden with sins, led away
with divers lusts, Ever learning, and never able
to come to the knowledge of the truth.
(2 Tim. 3:1–7)

With the inception of our American form of government
centuries ago, our forefathers instinctively knew the morality of good public policy, civil discourse, and governance
from policy that comes from an unenlightened society. Even
the unbelieving masses understood the difference between
the virtues of godly morality and the despair derived from
the shadows of darkness.

Our Christian forefathers' religious beliefs and their
moral convictions once radiated in the *public* halls of freedom and liberty. Most Christian public servants now cower
in the corner with fear. They rationalize their "eorean" view
of the state of the state (or state of the union for that matter)
pointing to the end times and the ultimate destruction of the
world and the ongoing deterioration of societal values. *In so
doing, they (we) have decided to play in a public policy sandbox
that has been designed by the world and is their unenlightened
version of how we are to conduct our governmental affairs.* Christians continue to underestimate and fail to understand the
depth and breadth of our civic responsibility to "redeem the
times" (Ephesians 5:16), to exercise control over (our
dominion responsibilities noted in Genesis 1:26), to direct
the affairs of (our stewardship responsibilities noted in 1 Corinthians 4:2), and lead (spirit-driven right of leadership
given us in Acts 1:8).

God has given us the "Genesis Mandate" of leadership in Genesis 2:15 as a model for our imitation. God told Adam to dress and to keep the Garden of Eden. We must labor sacrificially as servant leaders desiring to cultivate, provide, and protect God's creation as investors, not consumers. I believe that same model can be used in the political arena. Are you an investor or consumer of our government here in America?

For those who are willing to stand in the gaps and lead, we do so with an unfair advantage. We lead with the Spirit of God directing our paths. *We lead not by forging a superficial Christianity for political expediency. No. Christianity should never be considered a political strategy, it should exhibit life itself in the political arena through the fullness of abiding in Christ Jesus. Christians need to do more and push ahead with a renewed focus and commitment.*

4

SPIRITUAL WARFARE AND ENGAGEMENT

Please give me the strength to be as bold as a lion.

I STAND READY TO accept my part and to confess that I am guilty of negligence and sleeping at the wheel for the last 58 years. The material comforts of this life; the safety that pervades our individual spheres and social circles; the general application of the rule of law; and the predominant liberties of conscience that we currently enjoy have *softened our resolve to fight the spiritual warfare necessary to stem the tide of vulgarity in the political arena with all of its derivative forms.* Yes, there are many variations of vulgarity in our politics.

For the most part, we are a comfortable citizenry, enjoying the prosperity on the backs of those who came before us from an earlier day and time, unwilling to lay all at the feet of our Savior and pave the way for our children and our grandchildren. The Puritan Cotton Mather summed it up best, saying, "Religion begat prosperity and the daughter devoured the mother."[1] We have let the daughter of prosperity devour the holy and righteous nature of our Christian civic duties and responsibility.

Illustration 1.3

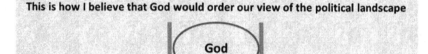

This is how I believe that God would order our view of the political landscape

God

Family

Church

Political Domain

The American principles that this country was founded on knew the appropriate hierarchy of authority and influence. God reigns supreme through the family unit and His church body, and that body is used to impact our politics for His glory. The subordinate position of the body politic is what America is missing and does not understand. We need to see the world with discerning eyes. Parents and Christian leaders around our country must get to work explaining these vital facts. Please (I am begging you) have a conversation with your child (student) about God's rightful place of ownership!

Illustration 1.4

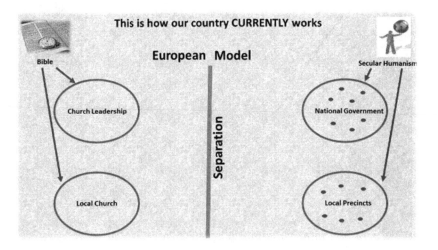

The Secular Humanist model, or what I will call the European model of how our government currently functions, is void of spiritual energy (the Holy Spirit is missing). The world despises God's moral law and will do everything in their power to nullify its effects. We know of the awesome power of God's Word when allowed to function in plain sight. We know that His Word will not return void. Can you imagine what would happen if the walls of separation between church and state came tumbling down? This country would have a revival that posterity would not soon forget!

However, the Bible's impact is narrowed in the current political arena in the United States of America. The world is trying to paint Christians inside the four walls of a church building, and we can't let that happen. We must use every lawful means available to defend our religious freedoms and determine to freely exercise those beliefs in all spiritual realms as the Spirit of God leads. We ought to obey God rather than men!

And while the separation of church and state limits our impact in many cases, we still have honest Christians trying to do their level best to redeem the times (the small dots in illustration 1.4 represent Christians fighting a spiritual warfare). Unfortunately, as discussed earlier, they are playing in the world's version of politics and the chances of them changing the landscape for our children and grandchildren is growing slimmer with each passing day.

---

[1] https://www.biblia.work/sermons/mathercotton/

5

OUR PURITAN
FOREFATHERS

*Please help me see, understand, and internalize the
aspects of Christian history that we need to carry
forward.*

THE EARLY PURITANS HAD an entirely different blueprint and
often used the phrase "stepping stones" in their description
of what they were trying to accomplish.[1] They wanted to be
spiritual "stepping stones" for all those who followed. They
wanted to pave a righteous path for posterity, which included their conversation and civic responsibilities.

Yes, their public service was informed from their deeply
held Christian beliefs, and they were willing to share those
sentiments at a moment's notice. They were in no way restricted or felt compelled to *only* share their religious and/or
public policy convictions when in environments of safety
and with those of kindred spirits. They were always ready
to share the hope that they had for a brighter tomorrow (Jesus Christ).

Their godly conversation and policy views were saturated with the moral law and standards of an Almighty God. God's moral law stood as their beacon of light. Aggressively voicing their opinions in the public arena (Bible opinions) was their standard practice. Jesus Christ and the Word of God were the stepping stones adamantly communicated toward the hope of building a Christ-principled nation. Pastor Jonathan Mayhew exclaimed, "You are assigned by Divine Providence, in the appointed order of things, the protector of unborn ages, whose fate depends on your virtue."[2]

Illustration 1.5

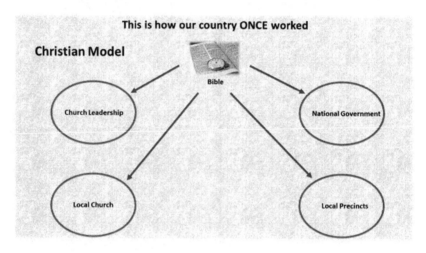

The historical and traditional view of our politics had the Bible right in the center, driving our country forward. God's moral law was revered by most of its citizenry during this period of American history and had enormous sway over every aspect of life. Because of the way we worshipped and acknowledged Him back then, great men who were spiritually minded helped shape and commission the Declaration of Independence and the Constitution of the United

States of America. These are documents for the ages that acknowledge the power of an Almighty God.

We are truly one nation under God. When Christians determined to live holy and righteous lives before Him and exercised those beliefs in all of the sandboxes of life, real change happened. These same principles and beliefs exist for us today. We simply must pick up the mantle for Christ and be determined to live every second of every day for the glory of God in whatever sandbox we happen to be in at the time. Stand tall and never let the world strip you of your Christian joy! Will you rise to the occasion and let God use you in the public service arena?

While the United States of America is a long way from Pilgrim, Puritan, and Colonial Christianity, we are still considered the flagship and shining light of everything that is free, decent, pure, and right. We are still one nation under God!

---

[1] Compilation by Verna M. Hall, *The Christian History of the Constitution of the Unites States of America*, The Foundation for American Christian Education (San Francisco, California, 1966), 177.

[2] Ibid.

6

A BLESSED NATION

Dear Lord, I want to be able to appreciate our great nation while fighting the spiritual battles necessary to keep our spiritual vibrancy.

WE ARE A BLESSED nation. The righteous hand of a holy God has seen fit to protect this great country of ours. The freedoms we currently enjoy are unparalleled in the annals of history. While our political conversation may be of an unseemly and harsh nature, God continues to bless us. We continue to be an ally and close friend to Israel. God will bless those that pray for the peace of Israel and want to be her friend (Ps. 122:6).

God also sees the millions of devoted Christian men and women who authentically want to serve a risen Savior and gather each Sunday to proclaim His name. It doesn't go unnoticed by our righteous King. We are doing so much that is good and righteous in the eyes of God. We must continue to break down the walls of separation between church and state (incorrectly and poorly defined, I might add) and resurrect the godly Christian virtue in the public arena.

We have a chance to change history and establish a new type of public service and leadership that enriches the foundations of our great country and restores her to her rightful place. I am proud to call the United States of America my country but am gravely concerned about the erosion taking place in our spiritual foundations relating to our politics. The best way for me to accurately describe the beauty of our great country and what it means to me is to relate two specific definitions from a book I recently published.

- A defined geographical barrier of protection for the freedoms and liberties of conscience that a sovereign God has ordained and so richly blessed us with that I am pleased to call my country

- A hiding place and a refuge for those seeking to experience the totality of freedom in the United States of America through the processes of entry appropriated and enforced by law[1]

---

[1] Michael J. LaPierre, *God's Gift of Imagination* (Houston: High Bridge Books, 2019).

7

Two Sandboxes

Please give me the wisdom to be able to communicate
a clear position on where we are as a nation.

NOW THAT WE HAVE identified our Bible-given responsibility
and looked at the cultural and historical implications, I
would like to describe the conditions of two separate and
distinct public service sandboxes.

The current state of public discourse and the ensuing
civic sentimentalities have reached a fever pitch that is un-
recognizable at any time in the history of our great country.
The experiment called the United States of America and the
democratic republic for which it stands is crying for want of
reprieve from the hatred and the vitriol being volleyed
about with such vigor.

The infused hatred in our public discourse cuts across
party lines and even cannibalizes its own when expedient to
preserve power, position, and the status quo. The Christian
idealism of fairness, justice, safety, and the moral authority
once emanating from the Word of God and displayed in our
political system is now seemingly beyond our grasp in the

spiritual and cultural realms of governance. The truths behind the deterioration and disintegration of our social and spiritual contract with God and one another, along with our civic responsibility, must be placed at the feet of those who are spiritually enlightened (His church).

We must not look to others who may have different policy opinions than we do and cry foul for want of someone to blame. We must not lament that the current conditions of public service are the result of the enemy's inroads and that it's "all their fault." Christian men and women need to self-reflect and scrutinize their individual roles in allowing the world (Secular Humanism) to crowd out the once highly esteemed Christian virtues inherent in our civil discourse and godly conversation of the past.

We must also stand ready to admit that there are times that we (His Church) bow to the policies of our political ideology at the expense of our Christian virtue which is found in His Word. The former must never be able to find a safe haven in the latter outside of His Word. In other words, Christians must never turn a blind eye to the delicacies of ideology (political thinking) when it is in direct opposition to God's moral law. Will you allow me to politely say, "Never, never, never."

8

THE CURRENT SANDBOX

Father, we are asking that you will give mercy and
grace to those public servants who are standing tall
in the face of adversity.

THE BEST WAY TO level-set the spiritual state of the union is
to lay down the overwhelming facts of where we are in public discourse and in Christian civic responsibility. Let's
clearly define and articulate the country's perception of
those who currently serve in a public capacity, along with
their respective motivations and what they hope to achieve.

In other words, what is the end game for many of our
public servants? The current sandbox is filled with Demo-
crats, Republicans, and a host of other parties desiring to
hold power, persuade, and impact the culture with their respective forms of government and public policy, i.e., party
platforms. They come from all walks of life, each wanting to
leave a legacy by effecting significant change in the United
States. They want to be revered, esteemed, and held to
standards and social standings that are much higher than
what we would consider to be an average citizen. They want

to be considered the elite of society. There is no disguising or mistaking their ambition. For the most part, their ambitious motivation rings loud and clear under the guise of service to our country. Quite frankly, they are serving themselves.

Let's consider a few one-word descriptors that additionally illustrate the perception that most Americans have of those who serve and the offices they represent. One has to wonder if we are describing the character traits of King Saul himself!

- Power
- Greed
- Inaction
- Self-Preservation
- Hatred
- Pride
- Elitism
- Gridlock
- Corruption
- Self-Serving
- Self-Self Aggrandizing
- Vitriol
- Compromise
- Grandstanding

REELECTION

To be fair, we must also recognize those uncommon leaders in our society who are selfless public servants who strive to remain above the fray of what it means to be a national, state, or local political insider. They are humble servants doing their best for their countrymen and even give God the glory on occasion. It is a blessing from above when we hear Christian public servants expressing hope in our Lord and Savior, Jesus Christ. There is no ego or sense of exaggerated self-worth in these uncommon individuals.

Beyond those few servant leaders currently serving in our government, what does the rest of society look like? How is society in general adjusting to the world's version of the political arena? Are they effectively "redeeming the time" and trying to restore our Christian responsibility to its former glory?

The easy answer to these questions would be to talk about all of the good that Christian men and women who serve in public and private leadership capacities do for our country and thank them for their service. We thank them for communicating clear Christian positions and standing up and fighting for the integrity and historical context of our rich Christian heritage. They stand tall and fight for life, liberty, and the pursuit of happiness. They use the Bible as their moral compass when making decisions.

We should recognize those public servants with a measure of commendation commensurate with the faith and dedication displayed. I truly believe this with all my heart! However, the more difficult answer to those questions demands a much more in depth, contemplative, and strategic determination when evaluating our current leaders' impact. In addition, we must also identify those specific leaders in society who can impact the masses for the cause of Christ on a larger and more personal scale.

Christians who serve in a public capacity, including pastors, deacons, elders, and those in other leadership positions need to realize that they are currently playing in the wrong public service sandbox. In many cases across our country, the Latin phrase, *Qui Tacet Consentrie,* may apply—translated, "he who is silent is understood to consent." Leaders must do more! We must not consent by remaining silent.

Illustration 1.6

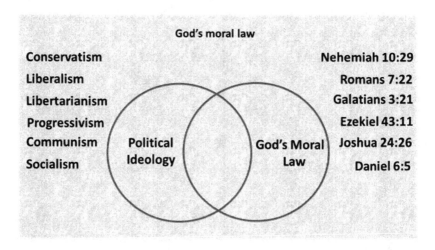

As Christians, we must live and breathe the moral law contained in God's Word. When there is overlap between God's moral law and our political thinking (our ideology), it certainly gives us a solid basis of discussion and a firm foundation for creating public policy and the corresponding party platforms. However, we must also be extremely discerning of everything that doesn't line up with His moral law, regardless of party affiliation.

We should be so full of godly wisdom and so grounded in His Word that our radars of discernment can pick up anything that wreaks of anti-God sentiment and policy. When we do pick up those anti-God sentiments, whether it be within the particular party of our choice or not, we must voice our displeasure and concern. As stated previously, when we remain silent, it appears to mean that we consent. We must never let the world think Christians are consenting to the forces of evil. From a Christian perspective, it would simply be an unAmerican position.

This country was founded on the principles of free speech, which still includes rigorous debate, discussion, and refinement on all of the issues, without respect of persons or party affiliation. When we do remain silent, we inadvertently support a position of absolute power, despotism, and dictatorship. The old adage "absolute power corrupts and power corrupts absolutely" applies in this hypothetical scenario of remaining silent. No human law should ever contradict:

a) The law of nature (God's law)
b) The law of revelation[1]

---

[1] Compilation by Verna M. Hall, *The Christian History of the Constitution of the Unites States of America*, The Foundation for American Christian Education (San Francisco, California, 1966), 143.

9

A WARNING

*May the seriousness of the situation cause
Christians to reflect and take action.*

THE WARNING IS PALPABLE. If we continue on our current
course and fail to right this ship, the country that we leave
for our children and grandchildren will look like every
other. There will no longer be an American and a Christian
distinctiveness. Christian virtue, morality, and ethics in the
political arena will all but disappear. We will no longer be
one nation under God. We will be a nation that serves a va-
riety of gods and resembles the conditions of Judah and Je-
rusalem under the early reign of King Hezekiah.

King Hezekiah understood the absolute travesty that
had taken place (and continued to take place at that time)
with the nation of Israel. He knew without question that Israel had forsaken the Lord God Almighty and set their
hearts on idols and other pagan distractions. He also understood that the path on which their forefathers had taken
them was leading to utter spiritual and physical destruction.

> For our fathers have trespassed, and done that
> which was evil in the eyes of the Lord our God,
> and have forsaken him, and have turned away
> their faces from the habitation of the Lord, and
> turned their backs. (2 Chr. 29:6)

Please understand, that the discourse today is not about supporting any kind of state-sponsored religion. No. I only have a vision where every citizen and elected official is boldly determined to express and exercise their religious beliefs in their civic capacities and in our political system without restraint. I believe our social and spiritual contracts with God and one another, along with our duty to help build a nation, demands our *further resolve.*

10

THE NEW SANDBOX

Please, Lord, give us the desire, clarity, and self-discipline to design an entirely new political sandbox that keeps the Constitution strong.

NEXT, WE WANT TO DISCUSS the new sandbox. What are the characteristics of this new sandbox that can give us hope?

The new sandbox is a gift from God. It is both a revival in the hearts of mankind (personal holiness) and a renewed spiritual energy in our political arena all at the same time. It is an arena that reorients its public conversation and civic responsibilities back to the Bible with a traditional understanding and involvement.

Christians decide to unite and redesign the entire public service landscape (new sandbox) under the influence of the Spirit of God. We shroud and build a hedge around our Constitution and Declaration of Independence with the impenetrable spirit of God's moral law. We decide that now is the time to take back control of the moral fiber of our country and bring it to the spiritual heights that only God Almighty Himself can do.

We submit as servant leaders; we obey the principles of God at all times; we fearlessly lead from the front with no regard for ourselves or well-being; we have no regard for position, rank, power, or societal standing; we engage in public discourse with the wisdom, grace, and ease that can only come from walking in the Spirit of God. Every conversation, every debate, and every discussion on the policy issues should be full of compassion and understanding with the intent of impacting His Kingdom. A kingdom is, of course, a form of political order. The Kingdom of God is one in which God is king, and clearly, God is a very different kind of king than King David or any other kings of the earth with whom we are familiar.[1] He certainly is a much different ruler than any we have in our country today.

Illustration 1.7

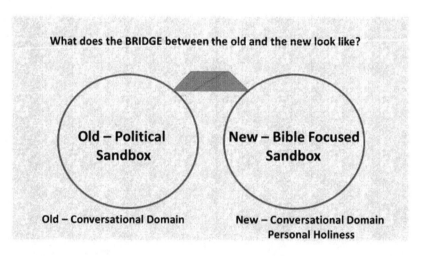

We need Christian men and women who are willing to defect from the grip of Secular Humanist servitude found in the old political sandbox and are willing to "put on" the new Bible-centric and God-honoring version of public service.

Refuse the one (Secular Humanism) and then fill our gas tanks with the blessings of the other (Bible version). Let's not miss the ultimate end of His vocational calling as citizens and public servants. That end is to love God and love people. The grace of God and the grace of faith will help change the landscape. The new sandbox is filled with Christian virtue and the fruit of the Spirit found in Galatians.

> But the fruit of the Spirit is love, joy, peace, long-suffering, gentleness, goodness, faith, Meekness, temperance: against such there is no law. And they that are Christ's have crucified the flesh with the affections and lusts. If we live in the Spirit, let us also walk in the Spirit. (Gal. 5:22–25)

While we will never compromise on any policy issues that are in direct conflict to God's moral law, we engage in those issues in an entirely different manner. We do so with a respect and collegiality for others that honors the positions they have been elected to represent. In other words, we talk to and respect one another as human beings. In addition, every piece of legislation (bill) that comes before our elected officials is evaluated in lieu of biblical, moral, and ethical standards and context. We go directly to the Bible and cite chapter and verse and herald those positions unapologetically.

We resolve our differences through justice, rigorous debate, and the rule of law. *We develop the technology necessary to link specific pieces of legislation directly to the Bible and other historical, factual, traditional, and precedent-leading insights that help condition our minds and our hearts to a Christian leadership worldview.* We also develop a relationship platform for engaging others that I will call *The Fundamental Orders of Christian Governance and Civic Responsibility.* We will use this as our guide to change the landscape.

Beyond this (as previously mentioned), we will continue to tear down the walls of Separation of Church and State through the appropriate legal channels and put the focus back on our individual freedoms expressed in the Bill of Rights. The freedom of religious expression must be front and center. We will clearly articulate the falsehood of the misconstrued intent of the separation clause found in the letter that Thomas Jefferson wrote to his Connecticut constituents. We will fiercely proclaim the freedom of religion expressed in the first amendment and the liberty of conscience that our forefathers so ardently supported.

We will continue to support and push legislation that allows public school children to fully take advantage of their ability to get off-site religious instruction through the Released Time programs in our state. Finally, we will propose legislation that brings the Released Time program from the shadows of obscurity to be included as mainstream high school course credit. The winds of change are blowing, and we need to do more as Christian leaders! If we were to add one-word descriptors for this new sandbox they would sound something like this:

- Civility
- Grace
- Love
- Respect
- Honesty
- Transparency

- Selflessness
- Humility
- Faith
- Morality
- Ethics
- Action
- Dependability
- Hope
- Results
- Vision
- Change
- God
- Leadership
- Service

TERM LIMITS

The real challenge for Christians is not in grasping and understanding the concepts of change in our political system. The real challenge comes in the execution of those responsibilities.

---

[1] http://www.stateofformation.org/2013/01/the-bible-and-public-policy/

11

FROM THE PULPIT

*Heavenly Father, we ask that you would encourage
pastors across America to stand up and lead in the
politics of our great country.*

MANY PREACHERS ACROSS THE United States of America are
also playing in the world's sandbox of Christian civic duty
and responsibility. For the most part, they remain silent and
are fearful, worrying that they will either offend someone in
the congregation or think they are breaking a law. Some pastors have even been so conditioned (indoctrinated) by our
culture that they believe discussions on public policy, civic
responsibility, and the role of government is not proper
from the pulpit.

Pastors need to be encouraged, uplifted in prayer, and
reminded that the only thing off-limits to them is unfairly
influencing the outcome of an election by endorsing or den-
igrating a specific candidate from the pulpit. Beyond that,
taking positions from the Bible and challenging believers on the
public policy and legislative issues of the day is well within

the purview of their ministerial roles. Christian attorney David Gibbs III sums it up best when he indicates that there are *no limits* when discussing issues from the pulpit.

In private, a pastor's personal views on the candidates is another matter entirely. Pastors can freely express their opinions in private. They are within their legal rights to do so. Please do not misunderstand my position here. I am **not** talking about having every service filled with policy discussions, legislation, or other aspects of public life. No, I am **not** talking about pounding the pulpit with an onslaught of political discourse. However, I am saying that pastors and all those in positions of Christian leadership in the United States must do more and lead our country. Who else can better articulate from the Bible what those civic responsibilities represent?

The Word of God is first and foremost a heavenly story about Jesus Christ. He is the author and finisher of our faith. In the Old Testament, we see the hoped-for Messiah in all of the various described "types" of Christ. In the New Testament, we read of prophecy fulfilled and the inspired depiction of Christ and His church.

However, the Bible is also a historical account of our Judeo-Christian heritage and one that comprehensively describes a compelling story about the process of *nation-building*. In the Old Testament, that nation-building process was focused mainly on Israel. Starting in the book of Genesis, we see human beings entering into vertical social and spiritual contracts with their Creator as well as horizontal social and spiritual contracts with one another. There were kings, judges, priests, prophets, and other leadership positions established to help them provide, protect, and govern for the good of the people. There is no getting around these facts.

In the New Testament, we again see a *nation-building* process but this time it is predominantly focused on the spiritual design of God's church. We are given hierarchies of authority and the roles and responsibilities of all those who God wants in positions of leadership. Christ lived in an eternal state of governance. He lived in an occupied land where ultimate political power rested with the Roman Empire and the proximate political power was the Sanhedrin (the Jewish court) that ruled over Israel. Since the Sanhedrin was a religious body, this meant that Jesus, like all Jews before Him, lived in a theocracy.[1] The relationships and key learnings gleaned from the theocracy of Christ's time and the democratic republic in the United States are linked and should be impressionably vivid. In other words, the civic leadership responsibility of pastors, deacons, lay people, and those in the political arena are all on full display in the Word of God.

I pray that Christian leaders everywhere will challenge, encourage, and show fellow believers what their specific biblical responsibilities are for being part of the *nation-building* process here in America. Yes, as long as we are considered a country, we are in an ongoing nation-building mode. In a democracy, we tend to think of partisan politics, but the actual word comes from the Greek *polis*, which simply means "the city-state." Politics is how we organize as a community; whether it is a democracy, theocracy, autocracy, or kingdom, it is still a political order.[2]

What our nation becomes in large part is derived by those who are willing to get involved and lead. If pastors and other Christian leaders across America are unwilling to lead in the area of Christian public discourse and civic responsibility, the only other option is to receive our instruction from the world and allow them to define our roles. Unfortunately, that is exactly what is happening across America. *However, it wasn't always that way.*

With little hesitation, preachers from yesteryear would engage in compelling discussion and debate about the church members' roles and responsibility in the public service sandbox. They were eager to help shape public opinion on the issues with a biblical perspective. Likewise, congregations eagerly anticipated how their pastors would respond to the specific social and policy issues of the day. Pastors were unafraid to engage on the issues and put their stakes in the ground either in private or in public conversation. They were unafraid because their stakes were heaven sent and supported high moral and ethical standards straight from the Word of God. Their stakes supported God's moral law.

The enthusiasm to lead out front on issues of governance has all but disappeared in our country. During the period surrounding the Revolutionary War, pastors were particularly vocal on issues and were eager to share them from the pulpit. Brothers and sisters in Christ, as a direct parallel, we should understand that we are in a cultural revolution, and it is one that desperately needs our attention, involvement, and leadership. Spiritual warfare abounds! I am not saying this to scare you or to paint a picture that might seem wholly magnificent and illusory in its proclamation. No. I share this with those of us who need to understand the depths of entanglement that our current system of public service has with the world.

---

[1] http://www.stateofformation.org/2013/01/the-bible-and-public-policy/

[2] Ibid.

12

THE SUPERHIGHWAY

Lord, we are pleading with you to give us a renewed vision of how this country should return to the days of old, when Christianity permeated every aspect of life, including our godly conversation, civic duties, and leadership responsibilities.

LET'S NOW TALK ABOUT the superhighway that will create the necessary convergence to lead our country forward:

> The highway of the upright *is* to depart from evil:
> he that keepeth his way preserveth his soul.
> (Prov. 16:17)

The superhighway connecting the current and new sandboxes is constructed with three primary components, which will provide the spiritual focus that will guide us along our way. The assumptions, *Fundamental Orders of Christian Governance and Civic Responsibility*, and the action plan that follows will help us consider "in our hearts that the LORD he is God in heaven above, and upon the earth beneath and there is none else" (Deut. 4:39).

However, we must also remember that all political orders should be judged against the Kingdom as a standard, an "impossible but relevant ideal" for which Christians are called to strive. This, then, is what Jesus has to do with public policy. Jesus invites us to enter the Kingdom, and by striving toward the Kingdom, we are irrevocably committed to striving toward an impossible ideal in our community life and our social and political order.[1]

The biblical mandates and principles that we will discuss should remind us to ring the bells of Bible reasoning and traditionalism in our political system every chance we get. In a sense, we become C.R.O.s (Chief Reminding Officers) to instill godly values and hope in all those who choose to follow. We need to constantly remind the world and each other what the true focal points of life represent. Congregations need to be reminded repeatedly about what the Bible says (vision) and the corresponding actions necessary to effect real change in the body politic. This journey will be long and arduous but filled with joy unspeakable and full of glory.

---

[1] http://www.stateofformation.org/2013/01/the-bible-and-public-policy/

13

THE PLAN

Lord, we ask for wisdom in how to proceed.

YOU WILL NOTICE THAT the first two bullets in each section of this chapter are the same. They are purposefully written to impress upon the readers the vital importance of prayer, personal holiness, and the impact of our words.

ASSUMPTIONS

- We desire and *pray* for personal revival and holiness that spreads a contagion across our state and our country (1 Thess. 5:17).
- The way that we speak and relate to people is filled with the grace and love of Christ (Prov. 25:11).
- Uncommon discipline will be needed for those who lead in this undertaking (Ezek. 22:30).

- Christians who engage with the spiritual energy needed to impact the culture and our political system will be greatly persecuted (2 Tim. 3:12).
- There will be significant human failure along the way as able Christian men and women will say and do things that are not in alignment with our founding principles that are based on His Word (Gen. 3:6).
- Moving from the current sandbox to the new sandbox is a process that will take generations (Eph. 5:16).
- Christian leaders desire to serve a cause much bigger than themselves, and that is the cause of Jesus Christ (Prov. 3:5).
- The news media will be against us and work overtime to disrupt our progress (Eph. 6:12).
- Pastors, public servants, and other Christian leaders across America have a renewed interest in leading our country in this biblical framework (2 Chr. 29:30).
- Power, pride, and self-preservation in the public domain is a recipe for continuing down a well-traveled and treacherous path of Christian annihilation in the United States and will be shunned at every turn (Prov. 16:18).
- We show no respect of persons in judgment but conduct ourselves in ways that are fair, firm, and with moral virtue.

THE FUNDAMENTAL ORDERS OF CHRISTIAN GOVERNANCE AND CIVIC RESPONSIBILITY

- We desire and *pray* for personal revival and holiness that spreads a contagion across our state and our country (1 Thess. 5:17).
- The way that we speak and relate to people is filled with the grace and love of Christ (Prov. 25:11).
- There is no king but King Jesus (Ps. 22:28).
- Our elected officials love God, and they love people (Matt. 22:37–40).
- The word politics is not part of our conversational domain (it has evolved to represent everything that is wrong with governance, and the use of the word must be avoided at all costs) (Matt. 10:16).
- Public service and leadership unto the Lord now redefine our mission (1 John 3:18).
- We die to ourselves (as Christ died for us) every minute of every day in the public arena (Rom. 6:12).
- In the hierarchy of authority, politics and governance takes its rightful place beneath Christ, the family, and His church (Acts 5:29).
- We strive for godly excellence in everything we do (Rom. 11:36).

- We are zealous supporters of the freedom of religion and have no desire to create a Christian theocracy as a state-sponsored government church (Eph. 4:3).
- We ardently support the United States Constitution and the Declaration of Independence.
- Our Christian radars of discernment (the Holy Spirit) must be increasingly sharp, as wolves in sheep's clothing will try to wreak havoc with our desired ends (Matt. 2:12).

ACTION PLAN

- We desire and *pray* for personal revival and holiness that spreads a contagion across our state and our country (1 Thess. 5:17).
- The way that we speak and relate to people is filled with the grace and love of Christ (Prov. 25:11).
- *Released Time Programs*, Good News Clubs, and other Christian nonprofits in public schools are key focal points that will help develop our children *toward* the things of God and away from things of the devil (Prov. 22:6).
- We must aggressively build relationships and alliances with those who support our cause (Prov. 18:24).
- We access news channels, social media, and other media outlets that will be sympathetic to traditional and biblical forms of governance (Neh. 2:7).

- We write voluminous op-eds to support all of our positions and circulate them (Prov. 25:25).
- We develop an entirely *new conversation* for public policy that relates everything back to the Bible (Ps. 19:14).
- We create innovative public policy apps and other technology platforms that are designed for a biblical worldview understanding and application for legislative initiatives (Ps. 119:16).
- We fervently sponsor and support faith-based and morally sound legislation (Ps. 40:8).
- We stand in solidarity behind the founding Bible-based principles of our new endeavor and renewed focus while minimizing lofty human thinking, expression, and communication that does not support our Christian ideals (Rom. 16:18).
- Church leadership must creatively design and emphasize a plan to inspire their congregations in their civic responsibility (annual emphasis month or week) (2 Pet. 3:1).
- We work tirelessly to the aforementioned ends (Prov. 6:6).

14

GOD'S MORAL LAW

Dear God, please enlighten our minds to a deeper
appreciation and understanding of your moral law
in a political-theological context.

IN THIS CHAPTER, we want to look at the importance of God's moral law in relation to the laws of the land. The functionality, utility, and practicability of written law can only be realized with its supreme and ultimate enforcement. Laws of a porous nature will not stand the test of time. Unwritten law, when duly enforced in its totality, becomes absolute authority governing the lives of those in its wake. The mores of civilized society have equal weight and a just balance of power helping to normalize the baser instincts of mankind. However, the exactness, prudence, and absolute nature of each (both written and unwritten) will *only* reign supreme when abiding in the attachment and consummation to the moral law of God Almighty. When formulating the laws of the land, we must never let the delicacies of political thinking and reasoning without God overshadow our commitment to God's moral law.

Furthermore, the legitimacy of our laws (written and unwritten) will only come by the consent of the people, by which they aspire to be protected, nourished, and developed to higher planes of moral, spiritual, and physical well-being. In addition, I would also argue that when brute force (in any of its derivative forms and subtle manifestations) is necessary in obligating one's constituency and citizenry to comply with the legislative, judicial, and executive dictates of the land, that authority is then rendered illegitimate and ceases to function as a recognized entity. Despots and tyrants heralding unenforceable proclamations and writs of compliance (executive orders) will always give way in the end to absolute authority that is shrouded in the precepts of truth, righteousness, justice, and holiness found in God's moral law.

Enforcement, consent of the governed, alignment to God's moral law, and an abiding affection and faith toward the laws of the land by its citizenry will procure a most favorable and long-lasting result that will be highly esteemed by posterity. Those nations living by this standard will be set apart with godly favor, heavenly significance, and earthly commendation even by those who do not share her passions or her resolve.

15

GOD'S CAUSE

Lord, we are asking for direction and confirmation by seeking your face.

WHAT ARE THE KEY INGREDIENTS of a just and righteous "cause" that can spur the emotions of a few, leading to unparalleled debts of compassion, commitment, and activism that can change the world? I believe that God uses the convergence of three separate and distinct forces of heavenly operation that produce an "other worldly" and spirit-filled comprehension of inspired events.

First, there must be *unity* of spirit. The Holy Spirit will *always* be the driving force of all just and righteous causes. The unity of Spirit I am referring to includes an appreciation for the spiritual gifts, thoughts, and contributions of *all* those committed to the cause. That unity also includes prayerful consideration for the principles, objectives, and praxis (the practice of our thinking) along with those called to participate and lead in this endeavor. There will always be an unparalleled rupture of spiritual conscience displayed in God-ordained causes.

Second, there must be union. The assembly and for-
mation of a just and righteous cause necessitates a uni-
formity and organizational construct that supports a lasting
commission. Furthermore, a grassroots energy should un-
dergird the soul components of our resolve. All kindred
spirits are welcome. When the people lead through
grassroots involvement and deliberative commitment, the
leaders will invariably take notice and follow.

Third, *harmony* has to exist at all levels. While the motivation of each participant to the inspired cause may vary
with the specific idiosyncratic nature of one's life and station
of progressive sanctification (their individual lanes), the
rapturous chorus of sweet harmony must permeate every jot
and tittle of the aforementioned covenant. We need to die to
self, put on the mind of Christ, and submit to a righteous
cause that is much bigger than any one individual. That
cause is Jesus Christ.

Fourth, the *timing and convergence* of the forces of this
heavenly operation should be determined with absolute certainty as the *call of God*. We *wait* with the patience of Job for
God's leading. We *think* with the wisdom of Solomon and
"consider it well" before fulfilling *our God-honoring commission*. We *act* with the certainty and veracity of Joshua to accomplish *God's will*.

16

SENTIMENTS FROM OUR CHRISTIAN FOREFATHERS

With all humility, authenticity, and truth, I can recommend no alteration or abridgment to the following quotes. These quotes are truly for posterity and the ages, thus reminded.

AND THUS THE AMERICAN republic, by illuminating the world with truth and liberty, would be exalted and made high among the nations, in praise, and in name, and in honor. I doubt not this is the honor reserved for us; I had almost said, in the spirit of prophecy, the zeal of the Lord of Host will accomplish this.

That her system of dominion must receive its finishing from religion; or, that from the diffusion of virtue among the people of any community would arise their greatest secular happiness; all which will terminate in this conclusion: that holiness ought to be the end of all civil government –

"that thou mayest be an holy people unto the Lord thy God."

If men, not merely nominally Christians, but of real religion and sincere piety, joined with abilities, were advanced and called up to office in every civil department, how would it countenance and recommend virtue! But, alas! Is there not too much Laodiceanism in this land? Is not Jesus in danger of being wounded in the house of his friends?

This will of his Maker is called the law of nature. For as God, when He created matter, and endued it with a principle of mobility, established certain rules for the perpetual direction of that motion; so, when He created man and endued him with free will to conduct himself in all parts of life, He laid down certain immutable laws of human nature, whereby that free will is in some degree regulated and restrained, and gave him also the faculty of reason to discover the purport of those laws.

The preamble to an early American Bill of Rights states,

The free fruition of such liberties, immunities, and privileges as humanity, civility, and Christianity call for, as due to every man, in his place and proportion, without impeachment or infringement, hath ever been, and ever will be, the tranquility and stability of churches and commonwealths; and the denial or deprival thereof, the disturbance, if not the ruin of both.' Here is seen, in the early American lawmakers, the influence of the Christian element.

For the strength of a nation, especially of a republican nation, is in the intelligent and well-ordered homes of a people. And in proportion as the discipline of families is relaxed, will the happy organization of communities be affected, and the national character become vagrant, turbulent, or ripe for revolution.

This influence is most visible and operative in a republic. The intelligence and virtue of its every citizen have a heightened relative value. Its safety may be interwoven with the destiny of those whose birthplace is in obscurity. The springs of its vitality are liable to be touched, or the chords of its harmony to be troubled, by the rudest hands.

This wholesale migration from the smiling fields of merry England to an unexplored wilderness beyond a thousand leagues of sea was of itself a most romantic and thrilling event, and when viewed in the light of its historic results it becomes clothed with sublimity. The men who undertook this work were not at all free from self-consciousness. They believed that they were doing a wonderful thing. They felt themselves to be instruments in accomplishing a kind of "manifest destiny." Their exodus was that of a chosen people who were at length to lay the everlasting foundations of God's kingdom upon earth.[1]

---

[1] Compilation by Verna M. Hall, *The Christian History of the Constitution of the Unites States of America*, The Foundation for American Christian Education, (San Francisco, California, 1966), 143.

17

Verses of Praise and Spiritual Clarity

Lord, may we live by your Word.

I EXHORT THEREFORE, THAT, first of all, supplications, prayers, intercessions, and giving of thanks, be made for all men; For kings, and for all that are in authority; that we may lead a quiet and peaceable life in all godliness and honesty. (1 Tim. 2:1–2)

Sing praises to God, sing praises: sing praises unto our King, sing praises. For God *is* the King of all the earth: sing ye praises with understanding. God reigneth over the heathen: God sitteth upon the throne of his holiness. (Ps. 47:6–8)

Let everything that hath breath praise the Lord. Praise ye the Lord. (Ps. 150:6)

Let them praise the name of the Lord: for his name alone is excellent; his glory is above the earth and heaven. (Ps. 148:13)

While I live will I praise the Lord: I will sing praises unto my God while I have any being. (Ps. 146:2)

Except the Lord build the house, they labor in vain that build it: except the Lord keep the city, the watchman waketh but in vain. (Ps. 127:1)

Let not thine heart envy sinners; but be thou in the fear of the Lord all the day long. (Prov. 23:17)

CONCLUSION

IN SUMMARY, the time has come for Christian leaders to submit to the authority of Jesus Christ relating to our public conversation, civic responsibility, and governance. The praxis of political theology fundamentally supports a *Christian leadership worldview*. We must have both clarity of vision from a saving faith found in His Word along with the necessary actions to impact the culture for His Kingdom.

Outside of Christ and His church, no other organizational construct (government) on this earth can further hinder our spiritual progress if left to its own device. A wild and untamed government that is void of spiritual depth and moral understanding will soon disappear. Let the soul leave the physical body, and all the parts of the body cease to function.[1] Let the Spirit be denied His place in the body politic, and the country ceases to exist or function as God has intended.

The only power that God recognizes in the body politic is the power of the Holy Spirit. All the rest is simply man's machinations, reasoning, and goodwill. On the other hand, an informed, passionate, and involved citizenry and congregation will act as a restraint on the ambitions of the uninspired portions of society who look to power, manipulation, coercion, and brute force to push their agendas. Christians will never have an impact on the culture for Christ unless we determine to be different. We (His church) must desire to create an entirely new public service sandbox and conversation for the glory of God.

Unity, union, and harmony will bring the necessary ingredients to engender a spiritual vibrancy that our community has never before seen. This is the new frontier of Christian conservatism in the political arena. I truly believe that the creation and execution of this approach to godly public conversation and Christian civic responsibility will ignite a public service zeal that is unparalleled in American history since the Great Awakening. I want to remind us of one important point. This is NOT a political strategy. This is a selfless commitment to lay down our lives (Acts 20:24) and do what is right for our children, grandchildren, and our countrymen. This righteous cause will take place when men and women commit themselves to personal holiness and decide to get involved.

Will you rise and stand in the spiritual gaps of history and be willing to fight for righteousness in all areas of our political responsibility? Will you endeavor to first ratify and then legitimize this covenant of citizenry with your prayers and your actions?

> That they may know that this is thy hand;
> that thou, LORD, hast done it. (Ps. 109:27)

---

[1] Compiled by Ron Eggert, TOZER for the Christian Leader (Chicago: Moody Publishers, 2001).

APPENDIX

*Lord, may the information in this appendix inspire
all Christian leaders in America and give us the
boldness of spirit needed to lead our country.*

POLITICAL SPEECH BY PASTORS

Pastors are permitted to engage in any political speech they
like as individuals. It is only endorsing a candidate on behalf
of their church that has been a disputed issue in the past.
When Lyndon Johnson was Speaker of the House in the
1950s, he passed legislation to punish non-profit groups that
had opposed him as a candidate.

Johnson's legislation prohibited non-profit groups from
endorsing candidates in an election and was not intended to
limit churches. However, that was the unintended effect
since churches are also non-profit organizations. Therefore,
since the 1950s, churches have been restricted from officially
endorsing candidates for election. No other political speech
was prohibited by either pastors or churches. The penalty
for officially endorsing a candidate for office was the re-
moval of the non-profit's tax-exempt status.

Although this legislation has tended to stop pastors and
churches from endorsing candidates, this legislation has

never been used to remove the tax-exempt status of a church. Some pastors, however, appear to like this legislation and use it as an excuse not to engage in any political activity at all to avoid offending members who might be on different sides of a political issue. Many pastors are apolitical and like to be able to say that the law prevents them from engaging in any political activity. While that is not correct, it does work for many pastors who want to remain apolitical.

Pastors who want to engage in political speech and activity, on the other hand, have always been free to do so. In fact, one of President Trump's first acts after taking office was to instruct the IRS not to penalize any churches for endorsing candidates by removing their tax-exempt status. Of course, the IRS had never done that anyway, but President Trump made it "official" with an Executive Order. Now Congress is also considering legislation to remove this candidate endorsement restriction from churches. In fact, black churches have done this for decades without any negative consequences, and many other churches are now doing the same.[1]

RELEASED TIME PROGRAMS

Released Time programs have been constitutional since the 1950s, when churches and other religious groups began to take students off campus after school for religious instruction.

Released Time programs have been around for over half a century and were held to be constitutional in 1952. However, they are sometimes ignored because they require a great deal of volunteer commitment and convenient meeting space outside the school building. In a Released Time program, the school board approves children to be taken from the school to another location, such as a church or private college, where non-school volunteers provide Bible lessons for the students.

Released Time programs peaked in 1947, with 2 million students enrolled in 2,200 community-sponsored programs. Currently, it is estimated that there are over 1,000 Released Time programs involving over 250,000 students in kindergarten through high school.

What is a Released Time program?

In 1952, the United States Supreme Court held in the case of Zurach v. Clauson that public schools may adjust their schedules to accommodate the spiritual needs of students through participation in Released Time programs, although this was not required. A Released Time program is implemented when students (with the written permission of their parents) are excused from attendance for part of the school day to attend hour-long sectarian religious classes at churches, synagogues, or other facilities away from the school campus.

Often, churches or other institutions, such as local Bible colleges, combine their resources to run the program. If the program is ecumenical, parents may choose which of several classes they wish their children to attend. Otherwise, a single church or local Bible college may sponsor the program for all students who wish to participate.

Subject to applicable state laws, schools have the discretion to dismiss their students for these off-campus religious classes. School personnel may neither encourage nor discourage participation by the students. Neither the students who attend nor those who remain at school may be penalized for their decision. During the class period in which the Released Time program is conducted (often the last period of the day or before lunch), the students who do not attend may be given a study hall or some other non-curricular activity.

Schools may not permit such sectarian religious instruction to take place on the school campus, nor may school personnel be used to teach such sectarian religious classes. The Released Time program must be taught by community volunteers and must take place away from the school campus. In South Carolina, schools are permitted to allow teachers to teach elective courses in religion; however, these are not technically released time programs.

How may churches or other community sponsors implement a Released Time program?

Released Time is the most under-used method by which outside groups can reach public school children for Christ. One reason that Released Time programs are so underused is that they can be difficult to coordinate and require numerous volunteers.

Schools boards must provide authorization for Released Time programs and should be requested to do so by the parents, students, and sponsors. Various courts have set the following standards for released time programs.

- School officials must permit notice of released time programs in the same way as community-sponsored little league or scouting events are announced. (Generally, the school board will distribute initial information about the program to all parents along with registration blanks and permission slips).
- Parents, churches, or other outside groups may conduct released time programs for public school students.
- Public school authorities must remain neutral with regard to the program.
- Students must be released for religious instruction upon the written request of the parent or guardian.
- Programs must be voluntary; no student may be coerced into attendance.
- Teachers and school personnel may not comment on attendance or non-attendance.
- Students may invite classmates to attend.
- Programs must not be conducted on school property.
- All students must be released at one time.
- Public school students may leave the school for no more than one hour per week to attend religious instruction offered by churches or other religious institutions.
- The religious instruction must be given by non-school personnel.

- The church or other religious body sponsoring the program must make weekly attendance reports to the school and must completely control the program.
- State officials may not monitor or judge the religious message.
- All costs and liability must be borne by the religious group(s) providing the program.
- The sponsoring religious group(s) must assume full responsibility for the students during this off-campus time.
- Classroom learning activities in the public school must come to a halt during this released time hour.
- The hour may be used by the schools for other clubs or study halls for those students not attending the released time program.

How may parents, students, and/or community sponsors obtain permission from the school board to establish a Released Time program?

In order to establish a Released Time program, parents must first request permission from the local school board. Before approaching the school board, parents and sponsoring religious organizations should have a well-developed plan with specific information about who will teach the program, how students will be transported to the off-site locations where the Bible instruction will take place, and how liability requirements and other costs will be met.

When the plans are completed, the group should schedule a specific time to present their request to the school board. Four or five articulate parents, students, or other sponsors should be selected to testify to the need for and interest in a religious program. The people who are going to present the request will generally need to register ahead of time to speak. They may do so by calling the school administration office before the meeting. School board agendas normally include an open agenda time when citizens can address the board.

Citizens who address the school board are sometimes granted only two or three minutes each to speak (unless the board has questions that extend the time), so the group should plan their presentation well. Printed material explaining the Released Time program and how it would work should also be distributed to school board members, the press, and the public.

The sponsors may need to be persistent. Depending upon the attitude of school board members and their interest in the program, several approaches may be needed. It may even require the election of new school board members favorable to the project to have the program approved. Petitioners should be sure to inform the local newspapers about the project in order to build community support and interest. Each local paper usually has an education reporter present at school board meetings.

As much as possible, the parents and sponsors who request the Released Time program should work closely with school board members in developing the concept. Since the school board is a politically elected body, the number of citizens who support the Released Time program will often influence board members regarding support or non-support for the project. The sponsors should attempt to collect petitions and have as many supporters attend the school board meeting as possible when the request is made. It is also helpful to have numerous students who support the program in attendance. The more support shown by the community and students, the more likely the school board will be to approve the idea.

Who determines what is taught in the Released Time program?

The individual churches or community sponsors determine how the program will be organized and what material will be taught.

Sometimes several churches work together, while other times the program is sponsored by a single community church or by some other community group such as a Bible college or children's evangelism group. In any case, after the program is approved and notices have been sent out and permission slips returned, the school has no further participation in determining how the program will be run. Such decisions are left completely to the sponsoring organizations. The sponsors determine what religious materials will be used, who the teachers will be, where the program will be held, how the children will be transported, and what special promotions, activities, or events will be included.

The Released Time sponsors are permitted to have either paid personnel or volunteers teach these Released Time programs. Sometimes churches will pay Bible college students to teach the program. Given the scope and cost of such a venture, the sponsoring groups must be particularly creative in their approach to providing funding, facilities, and personnel. When properly planned and carried out, these programs can be immensely successful.[2]

KEY COURT CASES

Here are the key court cases regarding Released Time programs:

Zorach v. Clauson, 343 U.S. 306 (1952)

The United States Supreme Court upheld the constitutionality of Released Time programs in which participating children go to religious classes held away from the public school. Released Time programs are constitutional if they are voluntary and are not sponsored by the school. In writing for the majority of the Court, Justice William O. Douglas said:

> We are a religious people whose institutions presuppose a Supreme Being. When the State encourages religious instruction or cooperates with religious authorities by adjusting the schedule of public events to sectarian needs, it then follows the best of our traditions, for it then respects the religious nature of our people and accommodates the public services to their spiritual needs. To hold that it may not would be to find in the Constitution a requirement that the government show a callous indifference to religious groups. That would be preferring those who believe in no religion over those who do believe. We find no constitutional requirement which makes it necessary for government to be hostile to religion and to throw its weight against efforts to widen the effective scope of religious influence.

Smith v. Smith, 523 F.2d 121 (4th Cir. 1975), cert. denied, 423 U.S. 1073 (1976)

The 4th Circuit court (which includes South Carolina) approved the practice of providing school enrollment lists to sponsors of Released Time programs even for elementary age students. The sponsoring group then used the student enrollment list obtained from the school to mail information and consent forms directly to parents. If the public school wants the Released Time program to use a particular consent form, the court held that it was permissible for the school to provide a sample form for use by the released time sponsor. After the parents fill out the parental consent form, the court held that the children are permitted to return the signed forms directly to the school.

Lanner v. Wimmer, 662 F.2d. 1349 (10th Cir. 1981)

Released Time instruction must be given by non-school personnel away from the school campus. The court considered it to be minimal involvement by the school to assist with the registration and record-keeping aspects of the program. However, the court did not permit the school to assume the task of regular attendance-keeping for the program after the registration and parental permission slip process was concluded and the students had returned their registration and permission slips to the school. The cost of printing and maintaining attendance cards is the responsibility of the sponsoring organization, which then makes weekly attendance reports to the school. The court held:

The registration and record keeping involved are necessary to administer the Released Time program and do not excessively entangle the government in religion or indicate the school's endorsement of the content of released time courses. The integration of the released time program into the public school schedule is nothing more than an administrative effort to accommodate the released time program with as little inconvenience to students as possible.[3]

RELEASED TIME IN SOUTH CAROLINA

South Carolina has been very favorable toward released time programs and has allowed them to be used for elective credits.

A case in South Carolina called Moss v. Spartanburg County School District No. 7, South Carolina (2012), protected the rights of students and parents to receive a religious education during school hours. Thousands of public school parents and children across the nation depend on released time classes so they can receive religious education from their churches, which the Supreme Court has allowed since 1952.

In 2006, South Carolina passed the Released Time Credit Act (RTCA), which allowed public school students the opportunity to take outside classes in religious instruction and receive elective credits. The classes are provided off-campus by third parties unaffiliated with the public schools. The RTCA made it easier for public schools to accommodate the religious interests of their students. In 2007, Spartanburg

County School District No. 7 passed its own policy permitting released time programs in compliance with state law.

In 2009, the Freedom From Religion Foundation sued the School District, claiming that the school's policy violated the Establishment Clause.

On June 29, 2012, the 4th Circuit unanimously upheld the program as constitutional stating, "[T]he program properly accommodates religion without establishing it, in accordance with the First Amendment."

In general, if elective credits are given, they should be offered to students in the same manner as other electives; however, teachers would not be permitted to urge students to attend.[4]

---

[1] https://www.ncll.org/

[2] https://www.ncll.org/

[3] https://www.ncll.org/

[4] https://www.ncll.org/

ACKNOWLEDGMENTS

I want to thank my wife (Calie) for being the first editor and keeping me balanced. With much patience, Calie has provided godly counsel and direction throughout this entire project.

I am indebted to both Dr. Carl Herbster and William Renfro for their "to the point" guidance for this manuscript. They gave me additional insight and perspective on the composition of this book that is greatly appreciated.

A special thanks to Darren Shearer and his team at High Bridge Books for their attention to detail.

I want to give a shout out to the local coffee shop in the town of Pickens, South Carolina, for allowing me to commandeer a spot for my laptop and set up shop for a while.

I appreciate the wise counsel and guidance of the National Center for Life and Liberty (NCLL) for their understanding of the rights of churches and religious organizations. For additional information, they can be reached at (888) 233-6255 or https://www.ncll.org/.

ABOUT US

Christian Leadership Worldview International (clwi.org) offers high-quality leadership training and development solutions at affordable prices. Our desire is to help grow leaders around the world one conversation at a time. We strive to impact organizations by improving employee morale, reducing turnover, increasing productivity, and fostering collaboration and teamwork as well as creating personal growth and self-improvement opportunities. In addition, CLWI takes a special interest in the development of young student leaders around the world.

Using a non-profit organizational model, CLWI has the flexibility to offer customized leadership solutions through a menu of options while being a low-cost industry provider. We are ready to serve the leadership needs of both employees and students alike. We are a Christian organization that uses Biblical principles and concepts as the foundation for organizational development and key learning experiences. Our focus is to point people to Jesus Christ, and we do it through training and development.

We believe that working through *local churches* is fundamental to who we are as an organization. As we help to grow Christian leaders on the one hand as well as evangelize and spread the gospel message on the other, we want to make sure that everyone is interacting with a local body of Christian believers as the Bible instructs us to do.

Our Logo

The prayer of Christian Leadership Worldview International (clwi.org) and its partners is that the logo represents a bold, compassionate, willing, and activist participant against a backdrop of global organizational need. CLWI wants our logo to signify the desperate need around the world for Christian leadership training and development in small-to-medium-sized organizations. We believe that many organizations today are being left out of this needed spiritual growth opportunity as they focus primarily on financial, social, environmental, and technological concerns, leaving out the spiritual development of their people.

The silhouette behind the podium in the logo depicts the "call to action" for Christian leaders to stand up and get involved. While leadership does not always mean being front-and-center in a crowd, it does mean teaching, training, challenging, and motivating people to reach new heights of spiritual development. From those who lead through prayers kneeling at a bedside to those who are called to preach and teach the Word in front of thousands, we must be willing to move beyond self for the benefit of others.